I0645678

The Cask of Amontillado

A Chilling Tale of Revenge, Deceit & the Dark Art of Burial Beneath the Surface

A Modern Translation
Adapted for the Contemporary Reader

Edgar Allan Poe

Translated by Tim Zengerink

Table of Contents

Preface
Message to the Reader

Rebuilding the Greatest Library in Human History

Thousands of years ago, the Library of Alexandria was the heart of global knowledge — a sanctuary where the wisdom of every known civilization was gathered and shared freely.

And then, it was lost.

Now, we're rebuilding it — and you are invited to join us.

At the Library of Alexandria, we've set out to make every book available to every person on Earth — not just in print, but in every language, every format, and for every reader.

Here's how we do it:

- **Deluxe Print Editions at True Printing Cost** - Order any book as a high-quality paperback, elegant hardcover, or stunning boxset — and only pay what it costs to print. No markups. No middlemen.
- **Unlimited Access to the Greatest Works** - Enjoy thousands of timeless classics — from Plato to Shakespeare to Tolstoy — in beautiful, modern eBook and audiobook editions. Read and listen without limits — for every reader, everywhere.
- **Modern Translations for Every Language & Dialect** - We're reimagining the classics in clear, accessible language — and translating them into every dialect imaginable. Everyone deserves to understand humanity's greatest ideas.

When you visit **LibraryofAlexandria.com**, you're not just accessing books — you're joining a global movement to restore, preserve, and share the wisdom of civilization.

Join us today at LibraryofAlexandria.com

Together, we'll ensure the light of human wisdom never fades again.

With gratitude,

The Modern Library of Alexandria Team

Visit:
www.libraryofalexandria.com
Or scan the code below:

Introduction

The Architecture of Revenge: Poe's Most Sinister Confession

Few stories in Western literature evoke a sense of cold, calculating vengeance as sharply and chillingly as Edgar Allan Poe's The Cask of Amontillado. Published in 1846, this brief tale of subterranean cruelty has mesmerized and disturbed readers for generations. It is a masterpiece of tightly wound structure, dramatic irony, and psychological precision. Though compact in length, the story echoes with themes of pride, deception, guilt, and the terrifying finality of death—a burial not just of a man, but of justice, conscience, and even moral clarity.

Set during a night of carnival revelry, The Cask of Amontillado introduces us to Montresor, a narrator whose first sentence sets the tone for the entire piece: "The thousand injuries of Fortunato I had borne as I best could, but when he ventured upon insult I vowed revenge." That declaration is chilling not only for its coldness, but for its ambiguity. What exactly was the insult? Was Fortunato aware of it? Was it real, or imagined? Poe deliberately withholds the reason for Montresor's murderous plan, and in doing so, he shifts our attention away from the victim's supposed guilt and toward the inner workings of the narrator's mind—a place darkened by wounded pride and a hunger for absolute retribution.

The story is narrated as a retrospective confession, addressed to an unnamed "you" who may be a priest, a judge, or perhaps even the narrator's own inner self. It is told with calm, eerie control, as if Montresor is recalling a work of art rather than a heinous crime. There is no remorse, no attempt at justification. Instead, the confession is a blueprint of perfect vengeance, executed with theatrical flair and infernal precision. Poe invites us not just to witness the act, but to inhabit the mind of the murderer. And in that invitation lies the story's deepest horror.

From the moment Montresor encounters a drunken Fortunato in the crowded streets, we enter a carefully staged performance. Montresor flatters Fortunato's pride as a wine connoisseur, dangles the possibility of a rare vintage— Amontillado—and manipulates him through a web of false modesty and reverse psychology. "I was silly enough to pay the full Amontillado price without consulting you in the matter," Montresor says, knowing full well that Fortunato's vanity will lead him to demand a tasting. And so, Fortunato, wearing the jester's costume of a carnival fool, is led into the darkness of the catacombs, unaware that he has already been marked for death.

The descent into the Montresor family vaults is more than just a physical journey—it is a symbolic plunge into the depths of obsession, revenge, and the death of moral clarity. As they walk deeper into the damp corridors lined with bones, the air thick with nitre, the atmosphere becomes suffocating. The setting itself is a character, amplifying the themes of decay, secrecy, and finality. The deeper they go, the more inevitable the outcome becomes, even as Fortunato—oblivious, coughing, laughing—plays along.

And then comes the moment of truth. Fortunato is chained to a recess in the wall, and Montresor begins to brick him in, one stone at a time. Even as the horror dawns on the victim, Montresor remains unmoved. His narration is clinical. The sound of the final jingling bells on Fortunato's costume becomes a haunting echo that stays with the reader long after the last stone is laid.

But the most unsettling part of The Cask of Amontillado lies not in its conclusion, but in its final lines. Montresor reveals that fifty years have passed since the murder, and still, the body remains undisturbed. "In pace requiescat," he writes—a Latin phrase meaning "may he rest in peace." Whether these words are offered in irony, mockery, or remorse is unclear. Poe offers no moral closure, only silence.

The Psychology of the Perfect Crime: Pride, Madness, and Control

Poe's genius in The Cask of Amontillado lies not just in his command of language and suspense, but in his intimate portrayal of a disturbed yet composed mind. Montresor is not a raving lunatic. He is rational, articulate, and methodical. And that is what makes him so terrifying. His calmness becomes a mask for madness, his elegance a weapon. He presents himself as a nobleman wronged, a man simply exacting what he sees as justice. But as we follow his actions, we begin to see that what drives him is not justice— but pride, wounded ego, and an obsessive need for dominance.

The crime is not impulsive. It is theatrical, ritualistic, almost sacred in its formality. Montresor's insistence on Fortunato's unawareness of the murder until the last moment reveals a twisted code of honor: "A wrong is unredressed when retribution overtakes its redresser," he says. In other words, true revenge must be undetected. It must be complete. Fortunato must die without suspecting Montresor's hatred. The silence around the insult is essential to Montresor's psychological framework. In his mind, revealing the motive would undermine the elegance of the act.

This attention to detail and psychological clarity mirrors Poe's own interest in the dark recesses of the mind. He was fascinated with monomania—an obsessive focus on a single idea—and many of his stories feature characters consumed by irrational but focused thoughts. In Montresor, we see a character whose entire identity seems to revolve around a single, private act of vengeance. He is not seeking resolution. He is seeking aesthetic perfection in the art of revenge.

But despite Montresor's control, subtle signs of guilt may exist. Why does he feel the need to confess after fifty years? Why record the story at all? The use of Latin at the end—"In pace requiescat"—could be interpreted as a prayer, a subconscious wish for peace, either for Fortunato or for himself. Poe offers no definitive answer. The story is a puzzle box with no solution, a confession that may not seek forgiveness, but compulsion.

The reader is left to wrestle with Montresor's psyche. Is he a cold-blooded killer or a victim of psychological torment? Is this the story of a just revenge, or a portrait of moral decay dressed in elegance and charm? Poe's refusal to provide certainty is what elevates this story beyond mere genre fiction and into the realm of psychological literature.

Buried Themes: Social Commentary and Symbolic Structures

While The Cask of Amontillado is often read as a tale of personal revenge, it also contains broader themes that reflect the anxieties of Poe's time—and our own. The setting of the story during a carnival, for instance, suggests a world turned upside down: a place of masks, misrule, and concealed identities. In this chaotic landscape, Montresor performs his crime with a sense of poetic symmetry. The chaos of the carnival becomes the perfect cover for a crime rooted in control and order.

There is also the issue of class and social hierarchy. Montresor and Fortunato are both noblemen, but their relationship hints at imbalance. Montresor's family motto—

"Nemo me impune lacessit" ("No one attacks me with impunity")—suggests an obsession with honor and legacy, perhaps compensating for a decline in status. Fortunato, by contrast, is rich, successful, and confident. His ignorance of Montresor's grudge may reflect not just personal obliviousness, but a kind of social blindness. He assumes his position protects him. Montresor proves otherwise.

This element of social tension adds a deeper layer to the story. Montresor's revenge becomes not just personal, but symbolic—a rebellion against insult, invisibility, or inequality. Poe, ever the outsider himself, may have used Montresor as a lens through which to explore the desire for recognition and the consequences of humiliation.

The story's structure also reflects symbolic dimensions. The descent into the catacombs parallels a descent into the unconscious. Each step deeper into the Montresor vaults mirrors a step deeper into repression, secrecy, and moral ambiguity. The bones that line the walls are not just reminders of death—they are evidence of a family history built on silence and burial. And Fortunato, bricked into the wall, becomes the ultimate buried truth—a metaphor for every insult, secret, or shame that festers when unspoken.

Even the wine—Amontillado—is symbolic. It represents temptation, deception, and illusion. It is the bait, the promise of pleasure, that masks the approach of death. That it may not even exist is part of the horror. Fortunato dies chasing a lie. And we, the readers, are left with a chilling truth: that sometimes, the deadliest traps are the ones we walk into willingly, out of pride, trust, or the desire to prove ourselves.

In this way, The Cask of Amontillado becomes more than a murder story. It becomes a meditation on the masks we wear, the grudges we bury, and the chilling precision with which vengeance can be carried out in the absence of empathy or redemption.

To read this story is to walk through a narrow tunnel of beauty and dread—where each step forward is another step toward the terrible unveiling of human cruelty. Poe does not offer a moral lesson. He offers a mirror. And in that mirror, we may see not just Montresor—but a part of ourselves that understands the cold, seductive logic of revenge, even as we recoil from it. Let us hope the final brick is never laid.

The Cask of Amontillado

I had endured countless wrongs from Fortunato as best I could, but when he dared to insult me, I swore to get my revenge. You, who understand my character so well, won't think that I made any threats out loud. Eventually I would have my vengeance; this was absolutely certain—but the very certainty of my decision ruled out any possibility of danger to myself. I had to not only punish him, but punish him without facing any consequences. A wrong remains unresolved when punishment falls upon the one seeking justice. It's just as unresolved when the person seeking revenge fails to make the wrongdoer understand that he's being punished and why.

I need to be clear that neither through my words nor my actions had I given Fortunato any reason to question my friendship. I kept doing what I always did—smiling at him whenever we met—and he had no idea that my smile now came from thinking about his destruction.

He had a weakness—this Fortunato—though in all other ways he was a man who commanded respect and even fear. He took great pride in his expertise with wine. Very few Italians possess the genuine spirit of a true connoisseur. Most of the time their passion is simply put on to match the moment and circumstances—to deceive wealthy British and Austrian collectors. When it came to painting and precious stones, Fortunato, like his fellow countrymen, was a fraud—

but regarding fine old wines he was completely genuine. In this area I wasn't much different from him: I was quite knowledgeable about Italian wines myself, and purchased them extensively whenever I had the chance.

It was around dusk one evening during the height of carnival season's wild festivities when I ran into my friend. He greeted me with overwhelming enthusiasm, since he had been drinking heavily. The man was dressed in a jester's costume. He wore a tight-fitting outfit with colorful stripes, and his head was topped with a pointed cap decorated with bells. I was so delighted to see him that I felt like I could have kept shaking his hand forever.

"My dear Fortunato," I said to him, "what a lucky encounter. You look remarkably well today! But I've received a cask of what's supposed to be Amontillado, and I have my doubts about it."

"How?" he said. "Amontillado? A pipe? Impossible! And in the middle of the carnival!"

"I'm not so sure about that," I responded. "I was foolish enough to pay the complete price for Amontillado without asking for your opinion first. You weren't around, and I was worried about missing out on a good deal."

"Amontillado!"

"I have my doubts."

"Amontillado!"

"And I must satisfy them."

"Amontillado!"

"Since you're busy, I'm heading to Luchesi. If anyone has a discerning eye for quality, it's him. He'll tell me—"

"Luchesi cannot tell Amontillado from Sherry."

"And yet some fools will insist that his taste is equal to your own."

"Come, let us go."

"Whither?"

"To your vaults."

"My friend, no; I won't take advantage of your kindness. I can see you have other commitments. Luchesi—"

"I don't have any plans—let's go."

"My friend, no. It's not the appointment, but the terrible cold that I can see is bothering you. The underground chambers are unbearably damp. They're covered with mineral deposits."

"Let's go anyway. The cold doesn't matter at all. Amontillado! You've been deceived. And as for Luchesi, he can't tell the difference between Sherry and Amontillado."

Speaking in this manner, Fortunato took hold of my arm. I put on a black silk mask and wrapped a cloak tightly around myself, allowing him to rush me to my palazzo.

There were no servants at home; they had left to celebrate the holiday. I had told them I wouldn't be back until morning and had given them clear instructions not to leave the house. I knew these orders would be enough to guarantee they would all disappear immediately once I was gone.

I removed two torches from their wall holders and handed one to Fortunato, then guided him with a bow through multiple rooms toward the archway that opened into the underground chambers. I descended a long, twisting staircase, asking him to be careful as he came behind me. Eventually we reached the bottom of the stairs and stood together on the wet floor of the Montresor family catacombs.

My friend walked unsteadily, and the bells on his cap jingled as he moved forward.

"The pipe," he said.

"It's further ahead," I said, "but look at the white webbing that shines from these cave walls."

He turned toward me and looked into my eyes with two cloudy, watery eyes that leaked the moisture of drunkenness.

"Saltpeter?" he asked, after a long pause.

"Saltpeter," I replied. "How long have you had that cough?"

"Ugh! ugh! ugh!—ugh! ugh! ugh!—ugh! ugh! ugh!—ugh! ugh! ugh!—ugh! ugh! ugh!"

My poor friend couldn't respond for several minutes.

"It's nothing," he said finally.

"Come," I said firmly, "we need to go back; your health is valuable. You're wealthy, respected, admired, beloved; you're happy, just as I once was. You're someone who would be missed. As for me, it doesn't matter. We should go back; you're going to get sick, and I can't take responsibility for that. Besides, there's Luchesi—"

"Enough," he said; "the cough is nothing serious; it won't kill me. I'm not going to die from a cough."

"That's right—absolutely right," I responded; "and I really didn't mean to worry you without good reason—but you should take every reasonable precaution. A drink of this Medoc will protect us from the moisture."

Here I broke off the neck of a bottle that I pulled from a long line of similar bottles lying on the moldy ground.

"Drink," I said, offering him the wine.

He lifted it to his mouth with a sinister grin. He stopped and gave me a knowing nod, while his bells chimed.

"I drink," he said, "to the dead who rest around us."

"And I to your long life."

He took my arm again, and we continued forward.

"These underground chambers," he said, "are vast."

"The Montresors," I replied, "were a great and numerous family."

"I forget your arms."

"A massive golden human foot on a blue background; the foot crushes a rearing serpent whose fangs are embedded in the heel."

"And the motto?"

"No one provokes me with impunity."

"Good!" he said.

The wine gleamed in his eyes and the bells chimed. My own imagination became heated with the Medoc. We had moved through walls of stacked bones, with barrels and large casks mixed among them, into the deepest chambers of the catacombs. I stopped once more, and this time I dared to grab Fortunato by his arm above the elbow.

"The saltpeter!" I said; "look, it's getting thicker. It hangs like moss on the ceiling. We're underneath the riverbed. Water droplets are seeping down through the bones. Come on, let's turn back before it's too late. Your cough—"

"It's nothing," he said; "let's continue. But first, another drink of the Medoc."

I broke open and handed him a bottle of De Grave wine. He drained it in one gulp. His eyes blazed with an intense gleam. He laughed and hurled the bottle upward with a gesture I couldn't comprehend.

I stared at him with surprise. He made the same movement again—a bizarre one.

"You don't understand?" he said.

"Not I," I replied.

"Then you are not of the brotherhood."

"How?"

"You are not one of the masons."

"Yes, yes," I said; "yes, yes."

"You? Impossible! A mason?"

"A mason," I replied.

"A sign," he said, "a sign."

"This is it," I replied, pulling out a trowel from under my cloak.

"You're joking," he said, stepping back a few paces. "But let's continue to the Amontillado."

"Fine," I said, putting the tool back under my cloak and offering him my arm once more. He leaned on it heavily. We kept going in our search for the Amontillado. We walked through a series of low arches, went down some steps, continued forward, and descended again until we reached a deep crypt where the stale air made our torches glow dimly rather than burn brightly.

At the farthest end of the crypt, another smaller chamber came into view. Human remains lined its walls, stacked all the way up to the ceiling in the style of the great catacombs of Paris. Three walls of this inner crypt were still decorated in this way. The bones from the fourth wall had been pulled down and scattered across the ground, creating a sizeable pile in one spot. Where the wall was now exposed after the bones were moved, we noticed an even deeper alcove, roughly four feet deep, three feet wide, and six or seven feet high. This space didn't seem to serve any particular purpose on its own, but simply filled the gap between two massive supports that held up the catacomb's roof, with one of the solid granite perimeter walls forming its back.

Fortunato raised his dim torch and tried in vain to peer into the depths of the recess. The weak light didn't allow us to see where it ended.

"Go ahead," I said; "the Amontillado is in here. As for Luchesi—"

"He is an ignoramus," my friend interrupted, as he stumbled forward unsteadily, while I followed right behind him. In a moment he had reached the far end of the niche, and finding his way blocked by the rock, he stood there stupidly confused. Another moment passed and I had chained him to the granite. On its surface were two iron brackets, positioned about two feet apart horizontally. From one of these hung a short chain, from the other a padlock. Wrapping the links around his waist, it took only a few seconds to fasten it. He was too shocked to fight back. Taking out the key, I stepped back from the alcove.

"Put your hand on the wall," I said. "You can't help but feel the saltpeter. It really is quite damp in here. Let me beg you one more time to go back. No? Then I absolutely have to leave you here. But first, I need to take care of all the small courtesies I can offer you."

"The Amontillado!" my friend exclaimed, still not recovered from his shock.

"True," I replied; "the Amontillado."

As I spoke these words, I kept myself busy among the heap of bones I had mentioned earlier. Pushing them out of the way, I quickly revealed a supply of building stones and mortar. Using these materials along with my trowel, I started energetically building a wall across the opening of the alcove.

I had barely finished laying the first layer of stones when I realized that Fortunato's drunkenness had largely faded away. The first sign of this was a low, groaning cry coming from deep within the alcove. This wasn't the cry of an intoxicated man. Then there was a long and stubborn silence. I laid the second layer, then the third, and the fourth; and then I heard the violent rattling of the chain. The sound continued for several minutes, during which I stopped my work and sat down on the bones so I could listen to it with greater pleasure. When the clanking finally died down, I picked up the trowel again and completed the fifth, sixth, and seventh layers without interruption. The wall had now risen almost to the level of my chest. I paused once more, and holding the torch over the stonework, cast a few weak beams of light on the figure trapped inside.

A series of loud and piercing screams, erupting suddenly from the throat of the chained figure, seemed to push me violently backward. For a brief moment I hesitated—I trembled. Drawing my sword, I began to feel around with it in the alcove; but a moment's thought reassured me. I placed my hand upon the solid stone of the catacombs, and felt satisfied. I approached the wall again; I responded to the shouts of the one who was crying out. I echoed them—I helped them—I exceeded them in volume and in strength. I did this, and the one who was shouting became quiet.

It was now midnight, and my work was coming to an end. I had finished the eighth, ninth, and tenth layers. I had completed part of the final eleventh layer; only one stone remained to be positioned and cemented in place. I wrestled with its heaviness; I set it partially into its intended spot. But then a quiet laugh emerged from within the alcove that made the hair on my head stand on end. This was followed by a sorrowful voice, which I found hard to identify as belonging to the distinguished Fortunato. The voice spoke—

"Ha! ha! ha!—he! he! he!—what a fantastic joke—an absolutely brilliant prank. We'll have plenty of good laughs about this back at the palazzo—he! he! he!—while we're drinking our wine—he! he! he!"

"The Amontillado!" I said.

"Ha! ha! ha!—ha! ha! ha!—yes, the Amontillado. But isn't it getting late? Won't they be waiting for us at the palazzo, Lady Fortunato and the others? Let's go."

"Yes," I said, "let's go."

"For the love of God, Montresor!"

"Yes," I said, "for the love of God!"

But I listened to these words in vain, waiting for a response. I became impatient. I called out loudly—

"Fortunato!"

No response. I called out once more—

"Fortunato—"

Still no response. I pushed a torch through the opening that remained and dropped it inside. The only sound that came back was the jingling of bells. The dampness of the catacombs made my heart feel sick. I hurried to finish my work. I pushed the final stone into place and sealed it with plaster. I rebuilt the old wall of bones against the fresh stonework. For fifty years, no living person has disturbed them. In pace requiescat!

THE END

Thank You For Reading

You've Just Read a Piece of the Greatest Library Ever Rebuilt

Thank you for reading.

This book is one of thousands we're restoring, reimagining, and translating as part of the **Modern Library of Alexandria** — a global movement to preserve and share humanity's most important ideas.

What was once lost to fire and time is now rising again — not just as memory, but as living, breathing knowledge, freely accessible to all.

What You Can Do Next:

*   **Keep Reading.**

    Discover more legendary works — in beautiful print, audiobook, or digital form — at LibraryofAlexandria.com.

*   **Build Your Own Library.**

    Every title is available as a paperback, hardcover, or collectible boxset — at true printing cost. Craft a personal library worthy of display.

*   **Spread the Light.**

    Share this book. Tell others about the movement. Help us translate every timeless work into every language, so no reader is ever left behind.

By finishing this book, you've already taken part in something extraordinary.

Join us at LibraryofAlexandria.com

Together, we're rebuilding the greatest library the world has ever known.

With appreciation,

The Modern Library of Alexandria Team

Visit:
www.libraryofalexandria.com
Or scan the code below: